WORDS BECOME ASHES

An Offering

Cindy Rinne

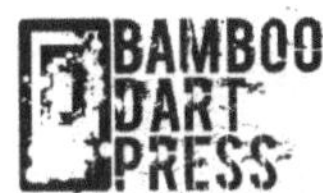

LOS ANGELES † NEW YORK † LONDON † MELBOURNE

Words Become Ashes: An Offering by Cindy Rinne

ISBN: 978-1-947240-24-7
eISBN: 978-1-947240-25-4

First Printing 2021

California Quarterly: “Riding the Wind”

Cholla Needles Journal: “Body Touching Stone” and “Closer to the Cosmos

Spectrum – Next: “View Next Door of Destruction”

Note: First line of “Riding the Wind” is the last line from *The Agnostic Folds Sloppy Hospital Corners*, “Psalter” by Georgia A. Popoff.

For information:

Bamboo Dart Press

chapbooks@bamboodartpress.com

Curated and operated by Dennis Callaci and Mark Givens

Bamboo Dart Press 010

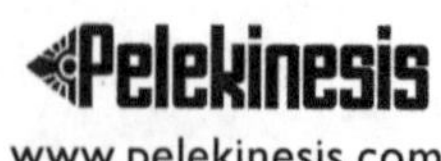

www.pelekinesis.com

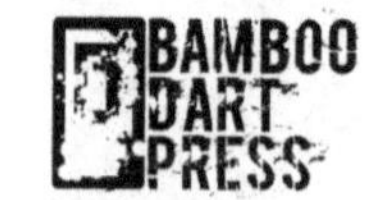

www.bamboodartpress.com

SHRIMPER

www.shrimperrecords.com

Contents

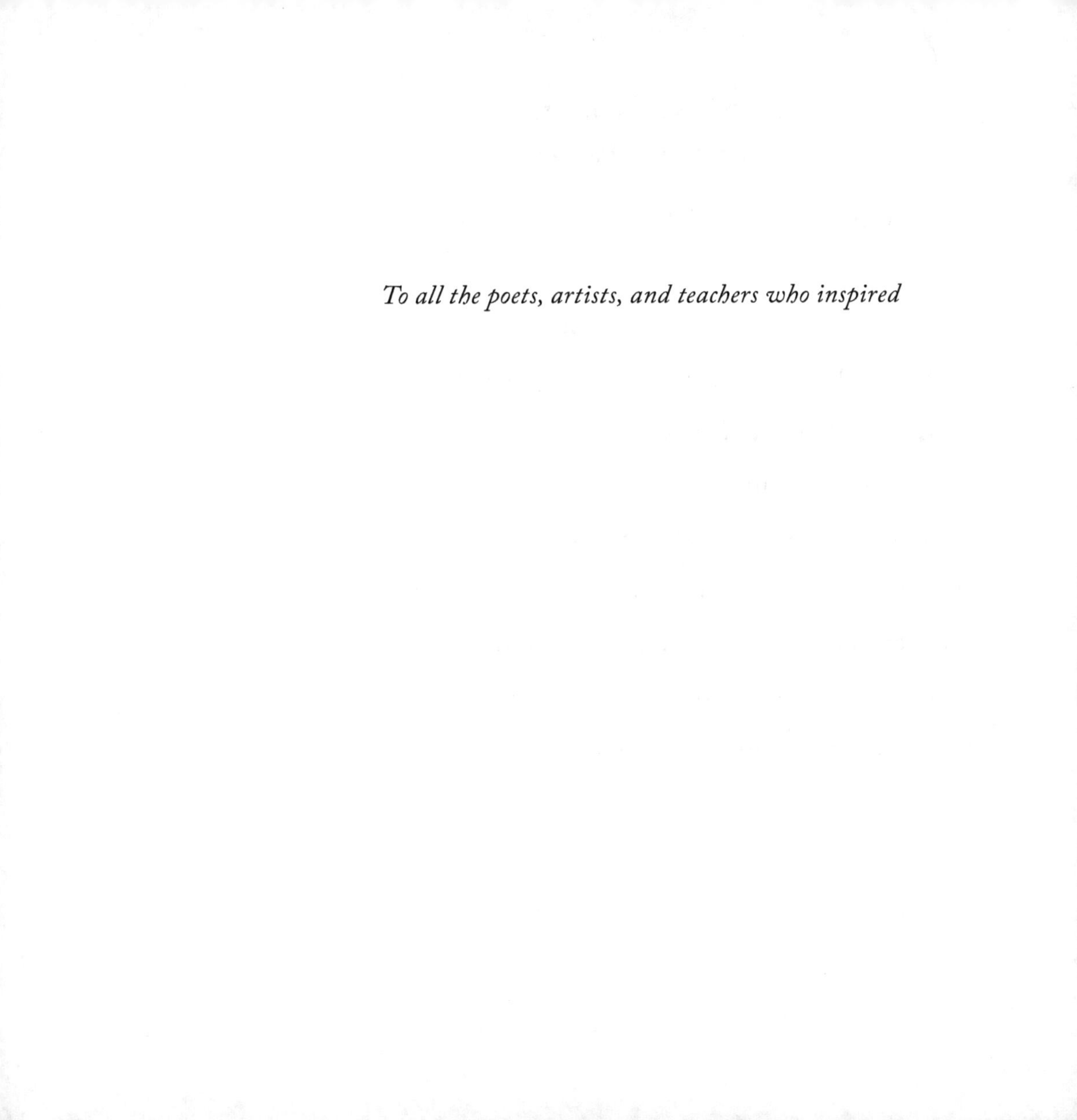

To all the poets, artists, and teachers who inspired

Dear Disappearance,

after Bushra Rehman

When the house burns, I fall from detached shelves
Find my lonely terra cotta skin a land map
of splotched embers   No noise within
my ocarina blood-spirit heart   The Queen of Heaven
unearths me from the smoldering singe
Egg-shaped head with an "O" mouth
I attempt a chorus for the alchemic royalty
My underbelly marks of triangles and checkered lines fade
Later her hands ask, *What does your body need*
I long for ashen trauma to transmute into music
Her fingers dance across as breath remembers

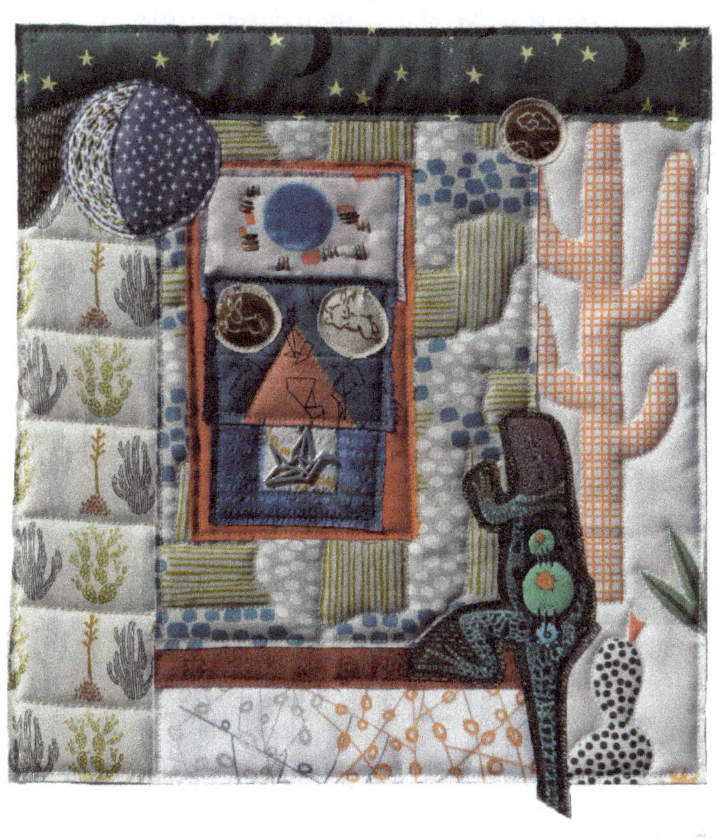

View Next Door of Destruction

Mole upcurves to a parched saffron surface.
Then burrows through misty sand, silt,
and clay. Unwinds forming a new path.
Giant roots anchor each turn—

I sigh.
Shadows hug.
A radiant crone appears
with long, white hair.

Stay rooted, underground for a while, she says.

On a pilgrimage, I follow mole; yet aware of the elder woman's
presence. Time to awaken senses other than sight to nourish
my heart. Move beneath the scenes like crawling through tunnels.

This Southern Magnolia, part of an ancient circle, surrounds a tall
vertical stone. Listen carefully and it sings a healing song.

The roaring of power saws when people refuse to hear.

Tree survived fire. Cut down today. Only sawdust left.

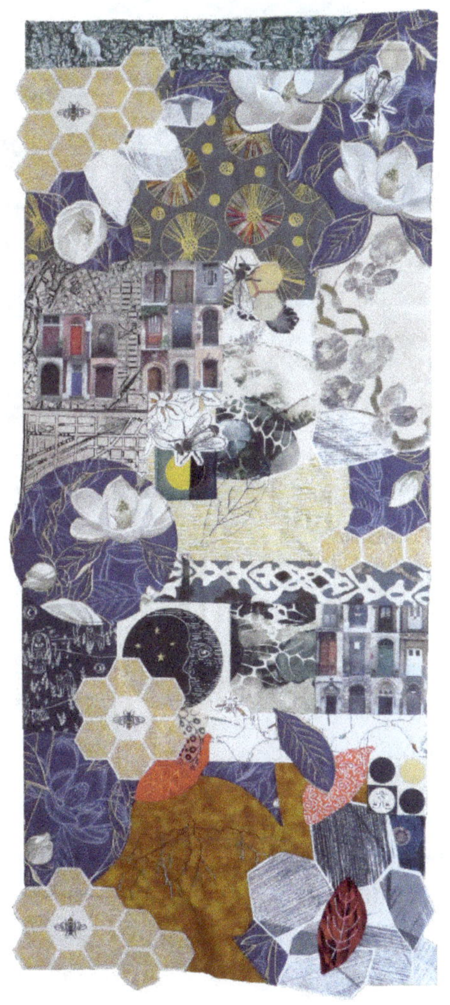

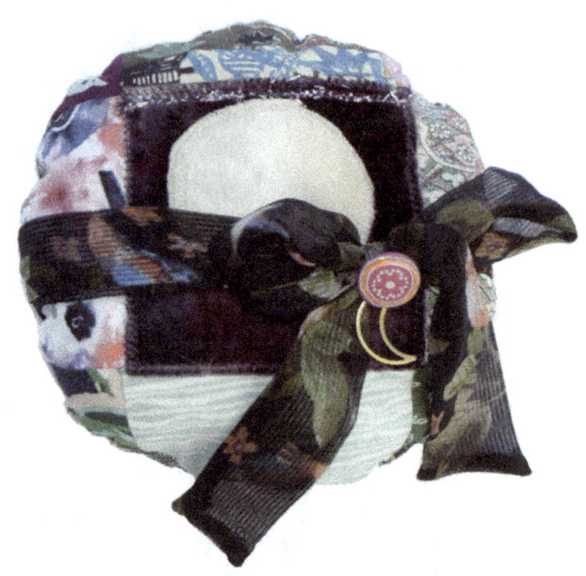

Fortune Teller

Peering
Down the tunnel

Columns outline my gaze
    A few graceful steps

I find an iridescent leaf
    Good for potions
    Rubbed on skin

Heron

Glides across the ceiling
Under purple moon

Forgets
    This is impossible

Pockets of light
    Orbs guide me

    To be involved
    In a conversation

With the bird—

They wonder
What forever means

Tears
Overflow my cupped hands

    I've avoided
    This place hoping to

Decay enough
    To understand

The ephemeral
    Flight of water

Riding the Wind

As I stand, turn, and fluff the pillows,
I find myself riding the wind
with a polar bear. Discovers they are not
separate from one another. This cold place

burns away pain and sorrow.

Douses with water to heal my heart chakra.
Now in a village, shivers as I wear
a crown of coral, citron, and obsidian stones.
The bear paints lightning, eagle, and mountain

symbols on my arms.

They join the circle and prance around the fire.
Flames conjure faces of a young woman
and a young boy. I bless the tribe
and retreat with the polar bear to nearby

mountains under gray moon.

I connect to my body. Dance between
worlds. A mystery to myself. Were they
the faces of my ancestors? Where do
I feel at home? I fill my lungs with

spaciousness of isolation.

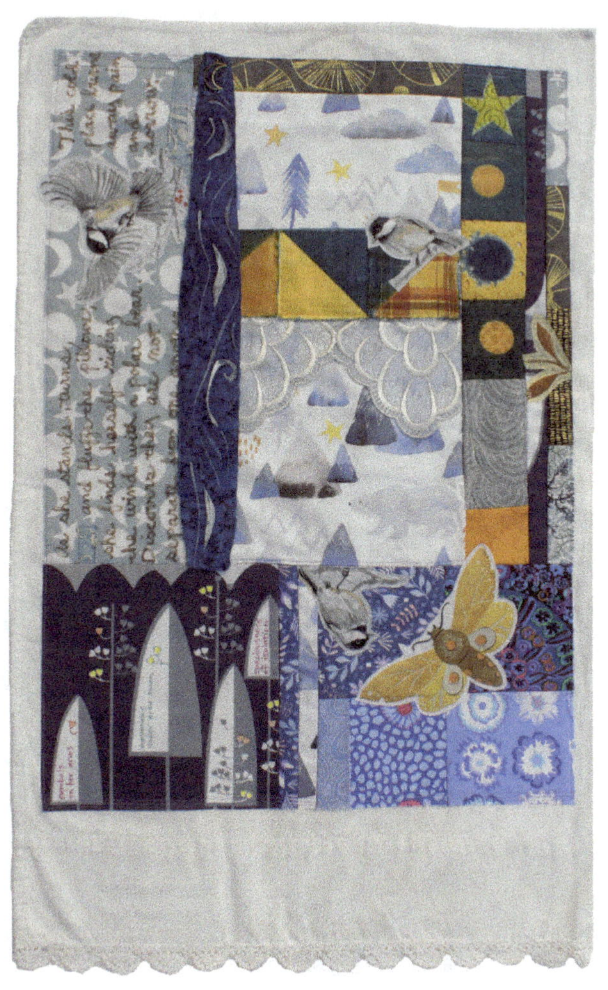

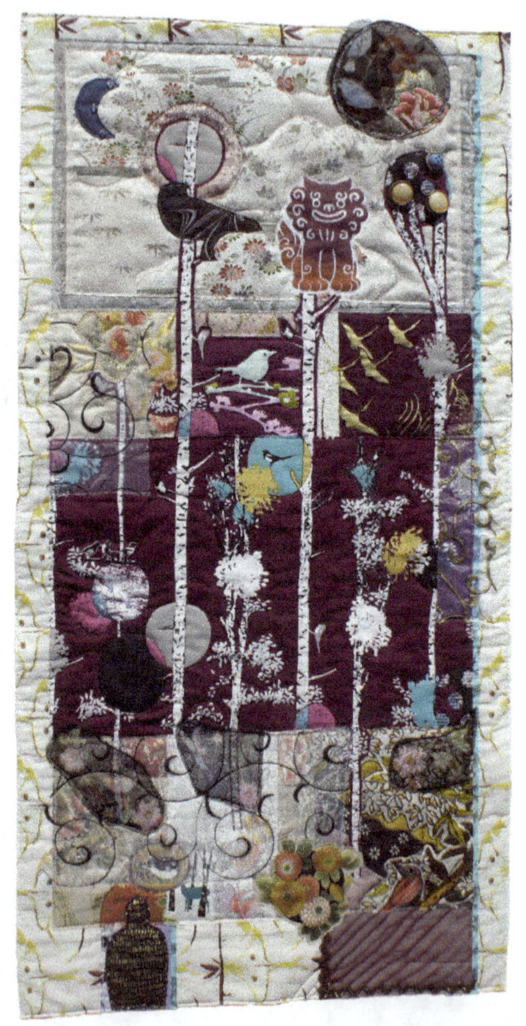

The Forest is Closed

No one at the visitor center since the forest is closed.
I park across the street. Through treetops I envision

a being with a fox head, then bird. Underneath the masks
reveal a blond woman floating. My grandmother

I never knew? She crochets a coverlet, a cross.
Shows me other women crafting by hand—

Clothing, weavings, baskets while they sit in a semi-circle.
I don't make a sound fascinated by their skills.

The other half circle consists of pines rustling in the wind.
Branches reach down to shake my hand. Cones rest below.

Sage and Indian Paintbrush sprinkle the mountain's
smoky light. One leaf scrapes and flips like cartwheels.

I discover oaks looming behind the pines. Great care
selecting an acorn gift. Downy Woodpecker, Dark-eyed

Junco, and Brewer's Blackbird chorus the women.
My heart pumps so hard it beats out of my chest.

Grandmother sings, *There's more than one way to see, to know.*

The shuttles pattern back and forth. I retrieve my heart and
old wounds in Mars retrograde with Virgo New Moon.

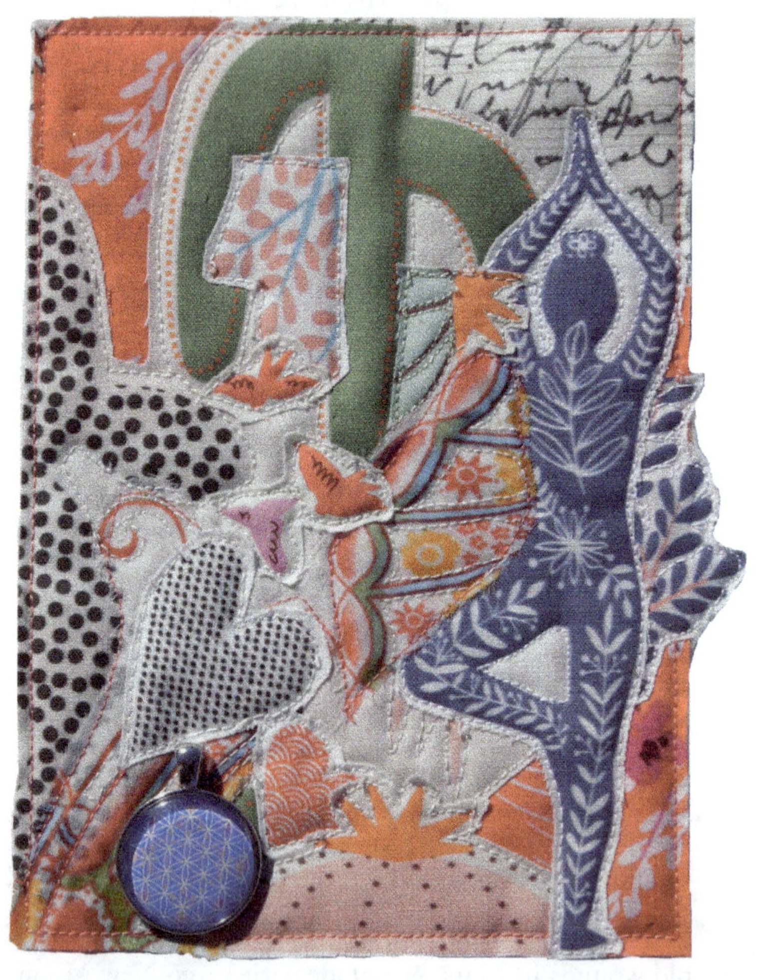

A Prayer

I am not alone. Pine, oak, birds, flowers,
women crafters in a circle.
Connect to myself and to others.

Ego is afraid. Burn that off to gain strength and
wake up the inner fire. Set my life on fire.
Let go of the pain and fear of the old story
for a new story. Pivot.

What deeply buried treasures are available to me?
Visionary creator. Truth-teller. Far-seer.

New wisdom to guide me. I am to share my treasures
and gifts with others. Radiant. Focus on my power,
wisdom, and beauty. **Empowered.** Resolution will come.
Be still.

Move in the body. Shaking and fluttering my hands
like leaves, like needles. **Tree pose.** Arms straight up.
Strong. Balance.

Quest

I turn upward and reach.
Minerva weaves wisdom
of her owl into my core.
Reframes the old stories.
She leaves winter rose behind—
I truly see.

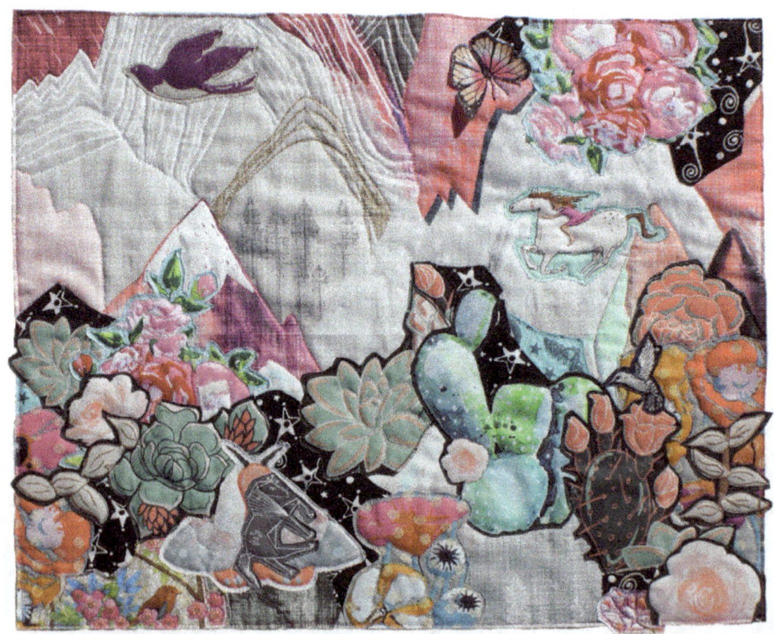

Dear Flood Plain,

Long ago, houses were built on your waterway. You responded with a flash flood – the way of water established long before stucco houses and fenced-in yards. The homes tumbled and were not rebuilt. I arrived when you were called "Private Property Keep Out." I sneak under the chain and listen to eucalyptus, greet the sunrise over the mountain, and take three deep breaths as my arms reach above my head. Wildflowers surround me. The foothills beyond them my view in one direction. Large houses still on either side. But in this wilderness, I have conversed with coyotes, watched hawks and ravens hunt, and once a chipmunk popped out of its hole chattering. I walk here often to sort out my thoughts or to be still before returning to the to-do list and traffic. Thank you for being there for me, an oasis in the city. On a clear day I can see across the land like you do and chant for the people.

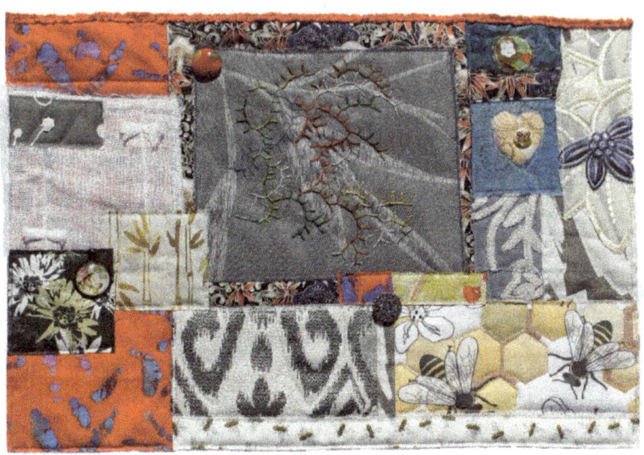

morphic

after Dakota Noot

I.
I meditate

large rabbit outer green ear
yellow & pink inside

a nude bird-man
stares cold
pierced hollow beak

II.
a black mound near the road
three large feathers
splay behind

head to one side
curls into body
wings touch breast

one straight leg
curved claw
grabs nothing

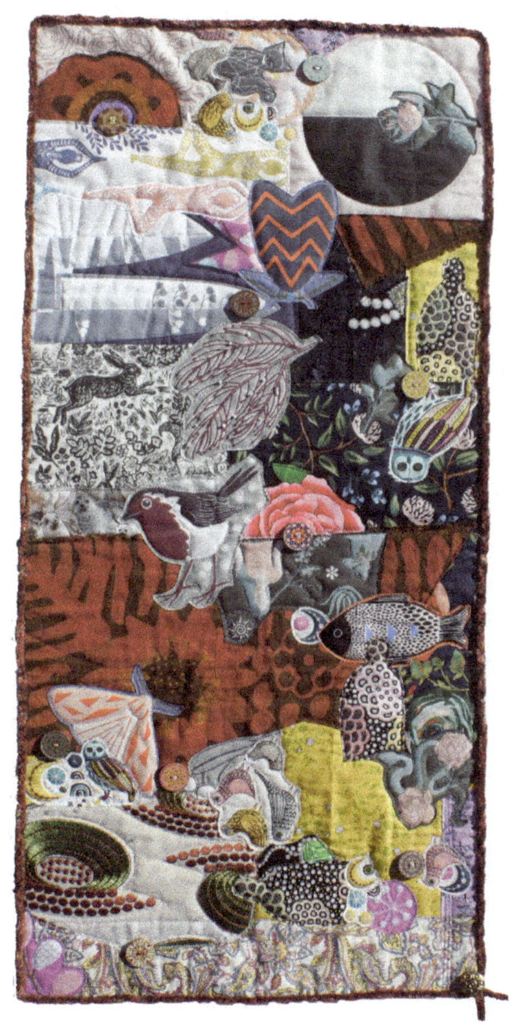

Body Touches Stone

As I walk towards healing, the Earth does too.

Karen Furr

Earth draws closer to the sun
    Willow flycatcher fits in my hand
    Feathers become ghost leaves
    A pottery jar floats in Whitewater River
    I lie down on stone shores
    In Serrano and Cahuilla lands
    Listen to the water through vibrations
    The splashes tell me to remake myself
A dying universe cannot create stars anymore

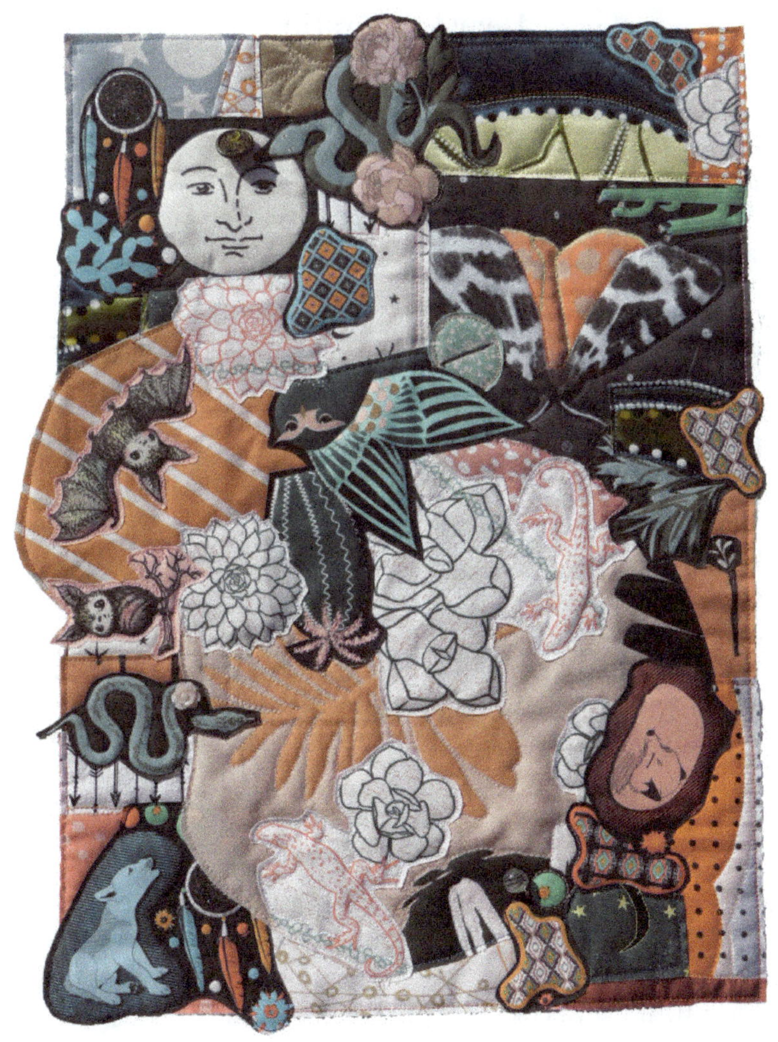

Dear Exploration,

after Amy Miller

Do you remember the small bowl
I retrieved
from the ashes? Burgundy on one side
and cream with brown splotches dripping
to the center.
Tiny handles. Burnt by flame, today holds rain.
Nearby, dwells the snake plant I selected from the nursery
when my backyard was barren.
I thought about how snakes scare me.
Do you think they are evil? The cause of our demise?
The gravity of these lies.
On my patio the lace of a drip system
waters the snake plant of green arms with black spots
decorated by the moon.
They open wide like a star
in a pot of free-draining soil
that dries between watering. This succulent
thrives in indirect sun. You will find it easy
to divide the roots of fleshy rhizomes.
I started several babies.
I already had my babies when the fire hit.
Grown up.
One left home for college; the other not far behind.
I lost their baby books. You had helped me

arrange their photographs of when they fit in their
father's hand.
Their childhood memories—
first pointe shoes and first ice hockey skates.
Young lives began after the burn.
Changing Woman asks, *Is there dirt*
in my belly? What trauma have I buried underneath
the minerals and organic matter?
Later, you found some baby photographs I had given you.
Returned them. In one my hair was dark brown
and my tummy large. A big smile on my face.
I wore a dress swirling
with bright colors and waved to the camera.
Film in those days.
I tear out the dead leaves. This creates room
for new growth.
Catch one thorn. Pluck it out of my hand.
Turn and see my reflection evaporate from
the half-filled bowl.

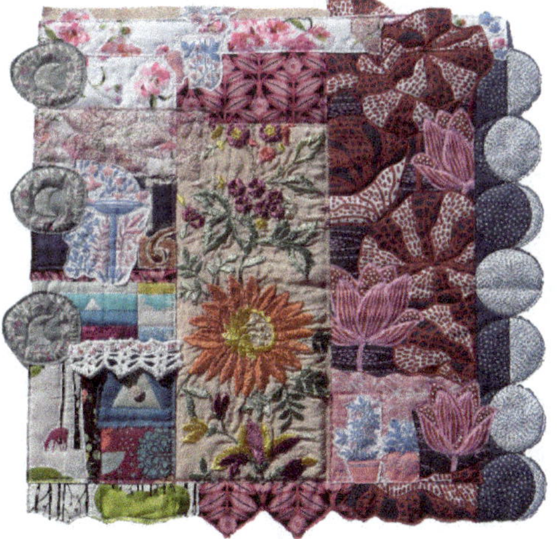

Apology

Sour desert sun
magenta base inclines
over golden tips

    wheat
    splits
    rends

a straight path

In solace
I walk on and on and on—

    clench
    an eagle feather
    a flute quivers

Sweet moon rises
like a circular window
Stars entomb the fire—

    self
    self-doubt
    self-rejection

hope apologizes at the bottom of my feet

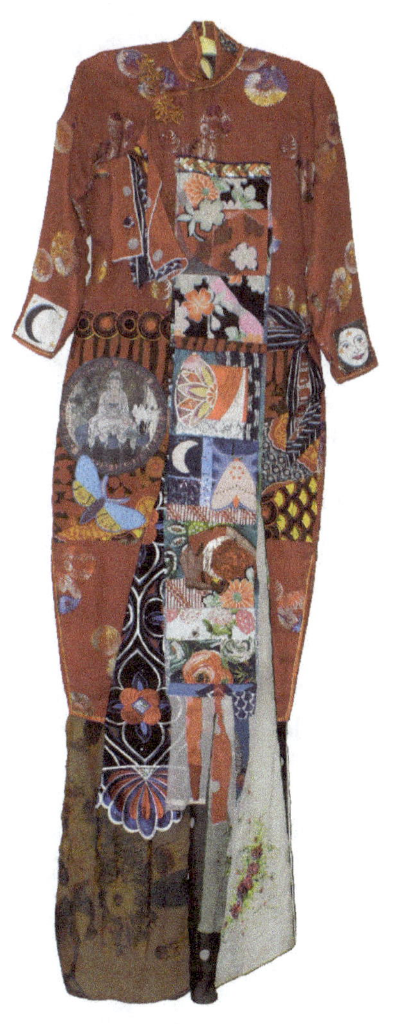

Held

Under Waning Quarter Moon, my giant
        larch shadow enters the cave
of mastodons, camels, and horses

painted in rust. A flame crackles
        from yellow to blue—
reflects in faceless women who wear

emerald necklaces and squat around
        the hearth, their heads held high.
Stars swirl above my shadow and

she adorns her neck with rubies—
        symbol of nourishing the heart.
Spirals through fire giving the faceless

women protection and visions. Holds
        a red jasper with flecks of olive
and gold. I sit outside the circle. My roots

grow into the soil. Branches trace ochre
        carvings of water rivulets
and repeating arches. A glacial river

strums outside the cave. My shadow sinks
        into the depth of Earth waters.
She ponders how horses ran free.

Above, I mirror her memories.
        The faceless women set a bowl
of holy water near the flame. My shadow

returns with roses. Each faceless woman
        breathes a word into her flower,
speaks it aloud, and tosses it into the basin.

I breathe the word "held" and clasp the scent
        over my heart as inherited thorns
clear from my womb space.

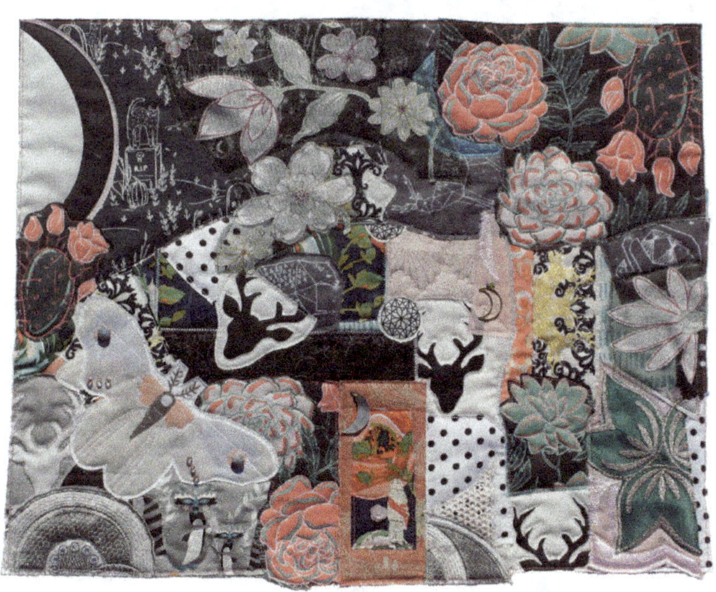

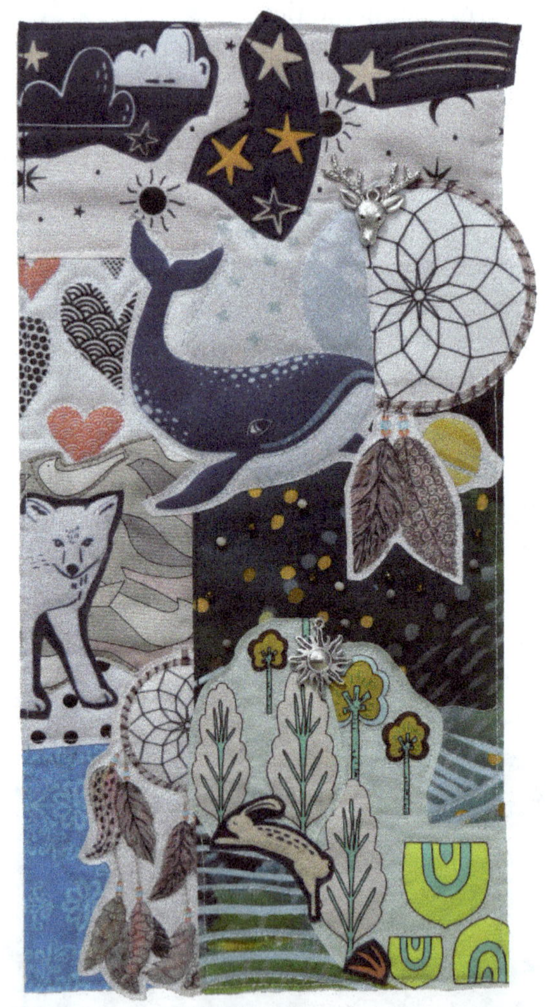

Closer to the Cosmos

What seems so distant dwells inside my body

a seedling of an unknown planet The birth of a moon
knits me to the upper world

I slow down to stitch a white dove
by hand Add crystals of earth and air
a thread trail lands at my feet

Knot deep abandonment sea waves etched
on stone

Sperm whales sleep vertically remember lineage stories

Caught in dreamcatchers woven in wire

Hanuman
offers protection as I chant the Heart Sutra
of spun wisdom

Tinkling melody of dark amethyst and metal wind chimes
Crocheted angels come near
with stars in their hands

Who am I?

Once I was a **witch** in the Black Forest. I rode
a cloud of knowing. Nightshades **summoned**
celestial energies. **Wolf** protected me.

I wore a bracelet of carved **scarab** stones—
tiger eye, carnelian, jade. **Amulet** of an ibis-
headed man helped **truth** to flow from my heart
as the sun was pushed into **existence** every morning.

Flying in a word map – rise of the **feminine**
with my unique **ability** to express moods
while overseeing nature's **patterns**
isolated in violet shadows.

I visited one of the six **realms** of rebirth
and saw a human who **nurtured**
the **world** as it collapsed with no real
loyalty to the **goddess**. My wolf bristled.

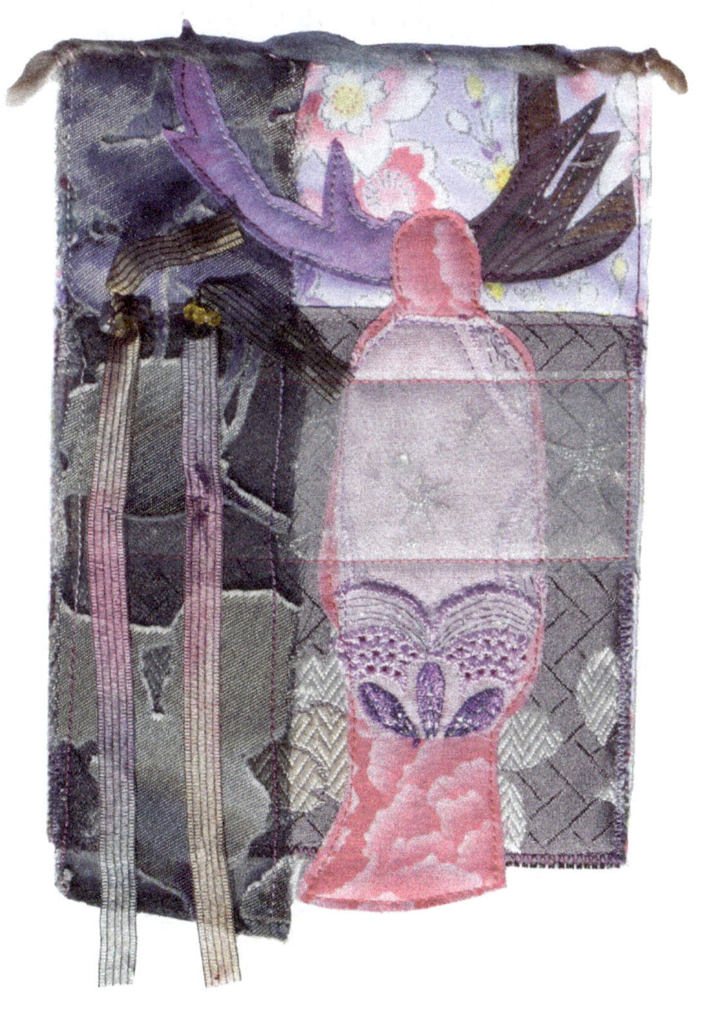

Words Become Ashes

Finding warmth in the distant star,
the light reveals an outsider
on a journey.

Illuminates the dark womb,
fears erased in a reborn
shadow-self. The vivid path
of recovery exposes labels
I believed. A goddess
guides me through the blue
door of perception and leads
to a monument of mint leaves.

What does grief look like?

Being seen. Having a name.
Merger of shadow and authentic
as I becomes the song of Raven.

Auk. Auk. Auk. Auk. Auk.

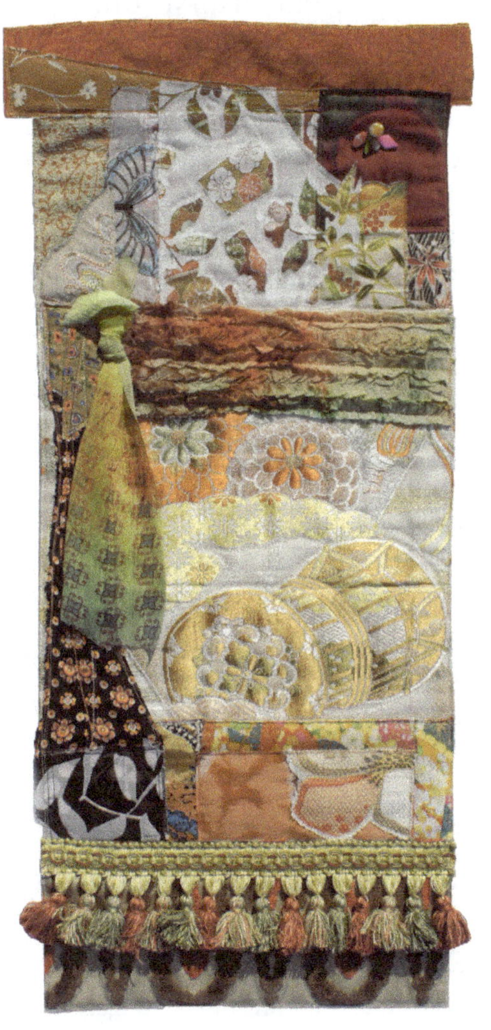

Dear Transition,

When you write of a fresh inch of snow—
here, the crows begin to caw and say goodbye
to winter. A murmuration
of starlings migrate and fill trees
of thin branches with the ruckus
of chaotic songs
as if they are tuning for the symphony.

Patient hawk
sits regal on the perimeter of my native plants.
Tiny birds gather a variety of grasses.
A movement in the corner of my eye
reveals a baby lizard, the color of sand.
Ancient face like an alligator.

It skitters across the coffee table and
inspects me. Watching icicles drip,
can you imagine rosemary
blossoms emanate musk as bees umbrella
with the mystery of hum?
Young pineapple sage leaves tinge my fingers

with their sweet, fruit scent.
Their sparse red flowers and
crumpled leaves hang on with
their last breath like Tibetan prayer flags.

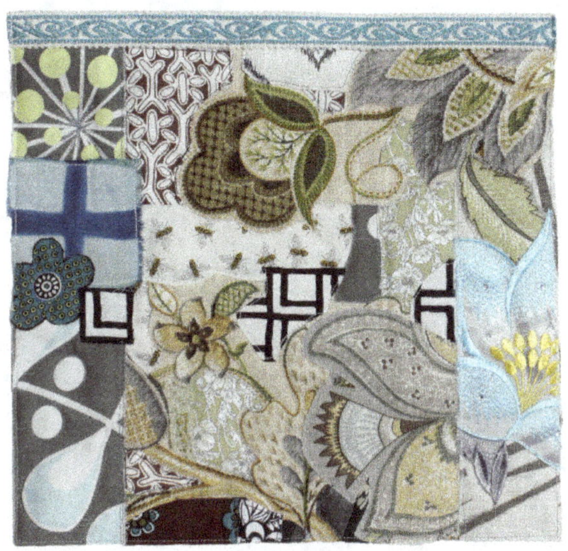

As the seasons change and circle—
mark the words that apply to you now:

Swallow – determination, commit to action, overcome adversity, faithful, new beginnings

Hawk – observe for a bigger perspective, study a situation before deciding, going in the right direction

Lizard – sheds skin, resilience, healing, survival, protection, let go of old patterns of the past, prosperity

Bee – fertility, wisdom, love, wealth, hard work, trust in miracles, balance, community

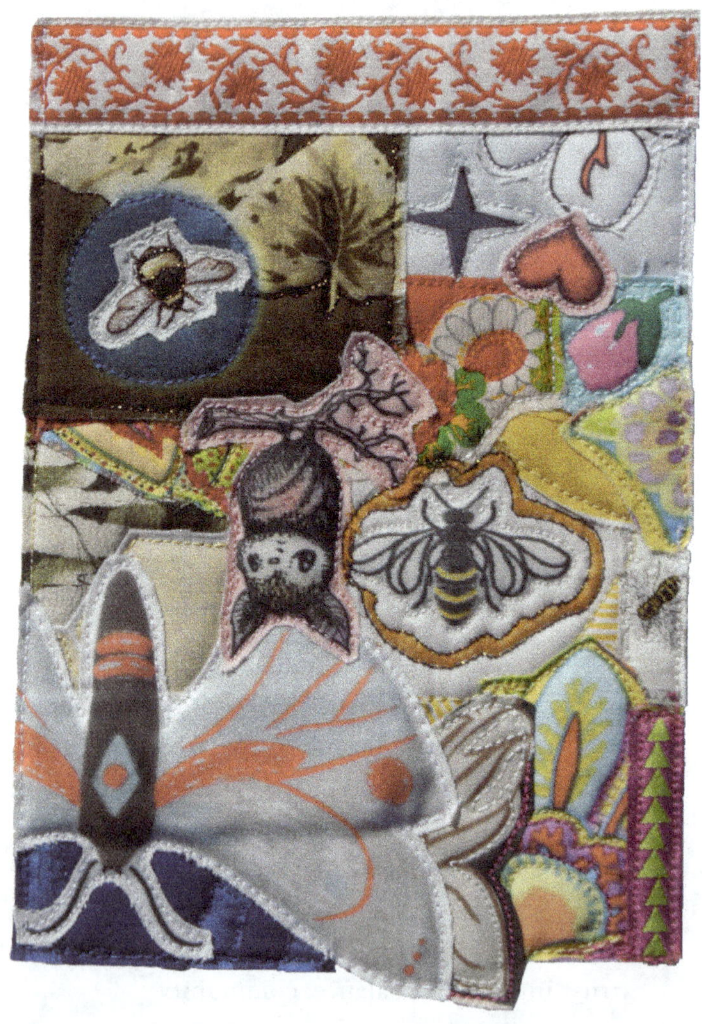

Visitations

I.

I stand at your roots
Reach out my hands
To touch your smooth
Underbelly where your
Bark has been eaten and
Ask how you are doing
During the virus?
You reply with
Follow the wind song
Gazing straight up
I feel small below
Your vast arms
Full of new spring
Leaves, guardian
Of the charred fields.

II.

I have a peace place – white lotus near a waterfall.
Picturing this quiets my busy mind. I add the idea
of allowing creativity to flow like the gentle pool
fed by the falls. A place holder for truth.
I am alone with nature and spirit. My voice quiet.

Dear Trauma,

after Heather Lowe and Bonnie Proudfoot

Sometimes life takes me
off the grid. Pulls me apart.
Glass, the color of raven
wings, tints of red and green.

Primal ooze. Did you see
my eyes disintegrate
while cast out by ashes?
Deposits energy into my body.
Open central core.

Look inside my spine.
Stored memories splinter—
a pulsing pain of purple
stabs through my back.
Diagonal energy rooting.
Polish the earth.

At the same time, I am
held by the universe
like a young plant
breaks through fire.
Survives.
Kiln-formed disc, a grid
in a circle for calm.

Observe my thoughts.
Don't judge or label them.
A place of rest and renewal.
I hold the ball of energy. Gratitude
present everywhere from my heart.

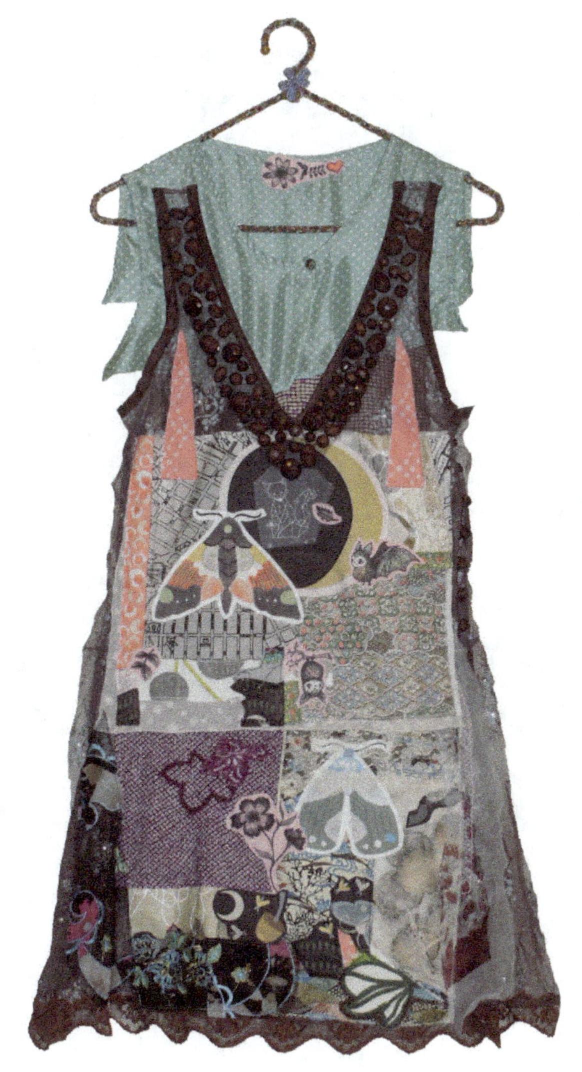

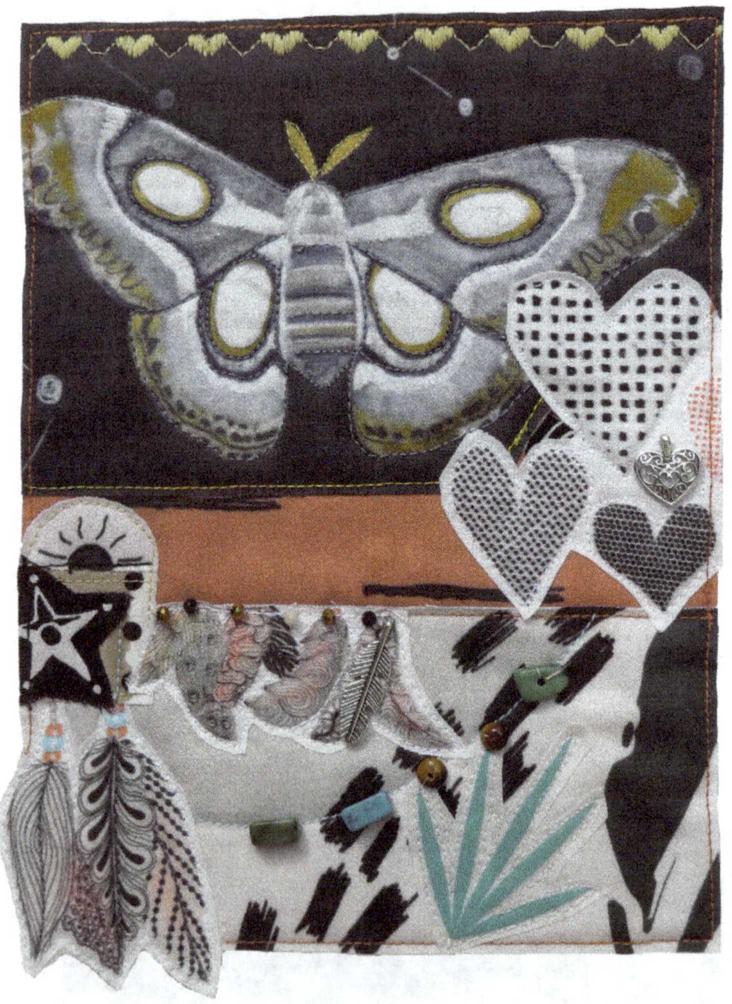

Nighttime Ritual

Add a pinch of organic sugar to homemade soy milk. Warm in the microwave. Sip slowly. Select clothes to wear the next day. Socks to accent or match. Wear PJs and do exercises for abs and Zumba to increase circulation. Breathe deep. Light two votive candles. Hope the neighbor's dog will stop barking by bedtime. Hold heart-shaped stone up to a candle where the glow shines through. Place the stone against my heart. Another slice looks like a nautilus shell. I rub this one across my back and shoulders – areas of tension. Night cream, vitamins, lavender oil, and brush teeth. Then stretch my back across a large exercise ball. Spray palo santo on pillow. Breath exercise closing one nostril at a time. Stand before the candles on chest of drawers. Stretch and bow before ceramic Buddha with thoughts of thankfulness for another day. Blow out candles. Smoke drifts to ceiling leaving lines like spider webs. Read about a small shoreline bird. Lights out.

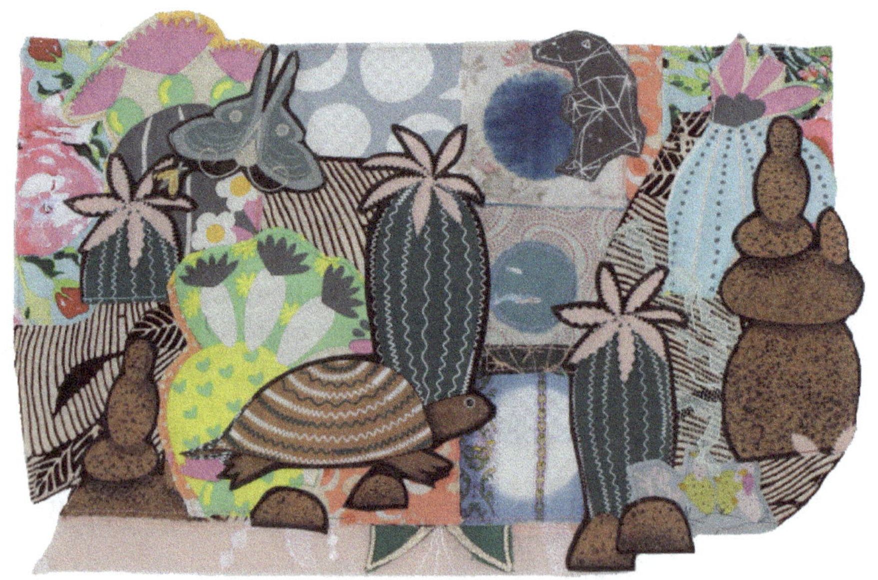

Silhouette

I.

Midnight high pitch sound
rub forewings in golden cage
my child gives them a name

II.

Flames of holiness anoint the air
of cassia and myrrh, a fragrance
singed with cinnamon and cane
Sparks dance rising—
A holy rite

Chants:
I am safe.
I am strong.
I am enough.

About the Author

Cindy Rinne is a San Bernardino artist and poet who has created fine art for over 40 years. She was Poet in Residence for the Neutra Institute Gallery and Museum, Los Angeles, CA. Her poems have appeared in literary journals, anthologies, art exhibits, and dance performances. Cindy is the author of several books: *Today in the Forest* with Toti O'Brien (Moonrise Press), *silence between drumbeats* (Four Feathers Press), *Knife Me Split Memories* (Cholla Needles Press), *Letters Under Rock* with Bory Thach, (Elyssar Press), and others.

She has participated in several online group exhibitions through LAAA/Gallery825. Cindy had tapestries in "Woven Stories" at MOAH (Lancaster Museum of Art and History) and at RAFFMA at Cal State San Bernardino for "Voices of Ancient Palmyra Resounded." She participated in "50/50, FIFTY/FIFTY, The Creative Magic of Collaboration" at the Progress Gallery, Pomona, CA. Cindy curated and exhibited at Chaffey Community Museum of Art and the Inland Empire Museum of Art. She exhibited with "Old Broads" curated by Karen Karlsson in several southern California galleries. She has exhibited at the Beatnik Lounge and La Matadora Gallery in Joshua Tree and is represented by Desert Peach Gallery in Yucca Valley, CA.

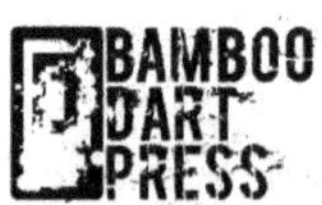

112 N. Harvard Ave. #65
Claremont, CA 91711

chapbooks@bamboodartpress.com
www.bamboodartpress.com

www.ingramcontent.com/pod-product-compliance
Lightning Source LLC
LaVergne TN
LVHW080333110826
845155LV00024B/155